Awaken
Your inner
Tsunami

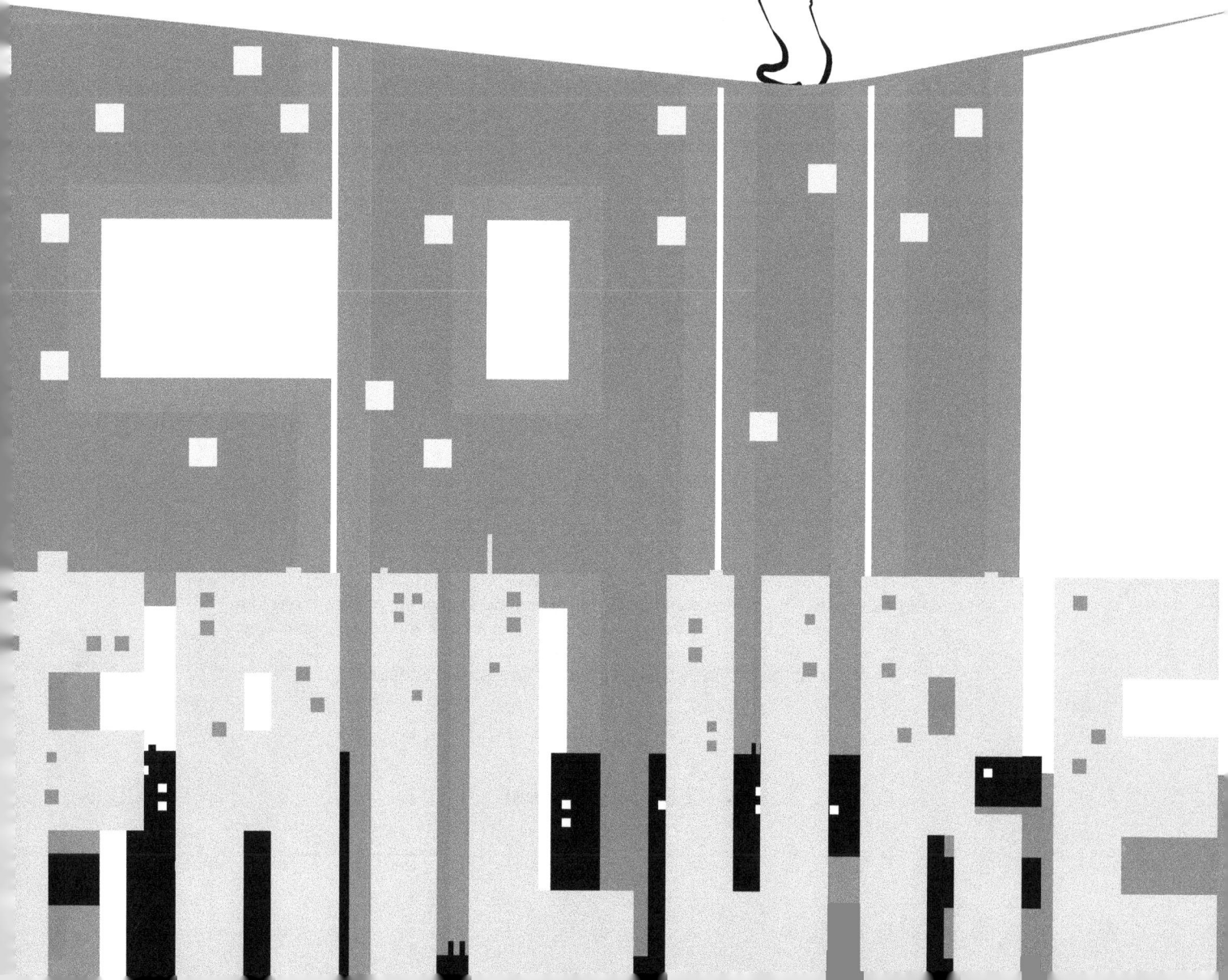

Cover Illustration by Garine H. Bekearian & Armen Sepetijan

ISBN-13:978-0692470794

ISBN-10:0692470794

Awaken Your inner Tsunami

A Motivational and Inpirational Fun Book for Adults

By Garine H. Bekearian

Awaken Your Inner Tsunami
A Motivational Activity Book for Adults

Can you find the characteristics of a strong personality in the grid below?

1- Confident
2- Optimist
3- Flexible
4- Hard Worker
5- Reliable
6- Fair
7- Responsible
8- Kind
9- Not weak
10- Realist

```
Q W G T N M S K F A I R G C T J D
R E S P O N S I B L E T R V Y G L
I H Y S O K N P F L E X I B L E
U A T J D G V C L Q A X N P
F S W H U I D C I L Z G
O R E A L I S T A Y E S
T O P F A R P F O R B I D
C A T J K D O V E G L U
T O I B U W O O N D E X R
M O M V C O N F I D E N T U P
H B I L F R B E R J S H A U N T
V I S K R K L O V E N G J L P
R T P B E Q P A T O F D H
O W J R K F P Y T
M O N E Y E G
```

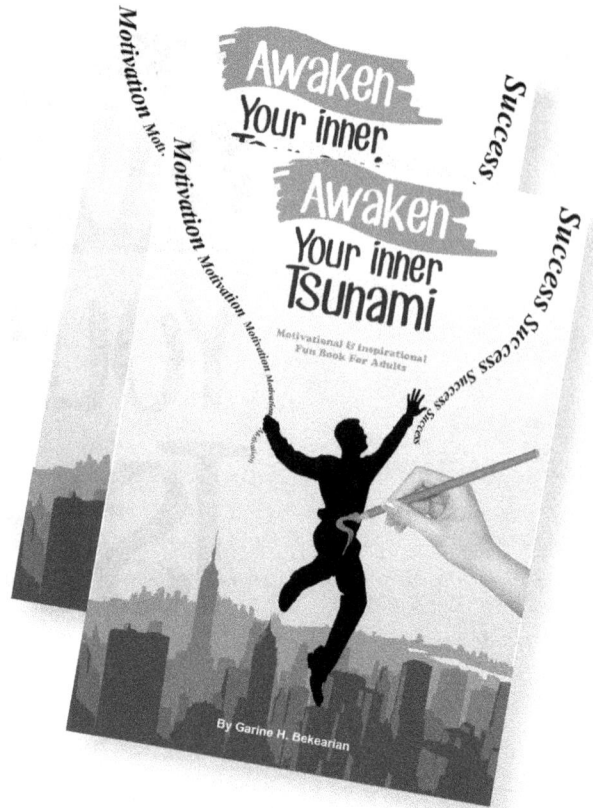

Can you find the characteristics of a strong personality in the grid below?

1- Confident
2- Optimist
3- Flexible
4- Hard Worker
5- Reliable
6- Fair
7- Responsible
8- Kind
9- Not weak
10- Realist

```
Q W G T N M S K F A I R G C T J D
R E S P O N S I B L E T R V Y G L
I H Y S O K N P F L E X I B L E
U A T J D G V C L Q A X N P
F S W H U I D C I L Z G
O R E A L I S T A Y E S
T O P F A R P F O R B I D
C A T J K D O V E G L U
T O I B U W O O N D E X R
M O M V C O N F I D E N T U P
H B I L F R B E R J S H A U N T
V I S K R K L O V E N G J L P
R T P B E Q P A T O F D H
O W J R K F P Y T
M O N E Y E G
```

Answer Key

You will find the answers to the games on page 32. No cheating!:)

Whether you want to succeed in your career or become the person you have always dreamed of, or get in shape, or maybe quit a bad habit like cigarettes and drugs, or maybe become a millionaire... This book offers you some motivation to achieve your goal while having you some fun.

"Because it's not about the money, it's about the best you can be"
Gary Keller

It's not about what others think, it's about the best you can be!
Are you ready??

Can you find the characteristics of a strong personality in the grid below?

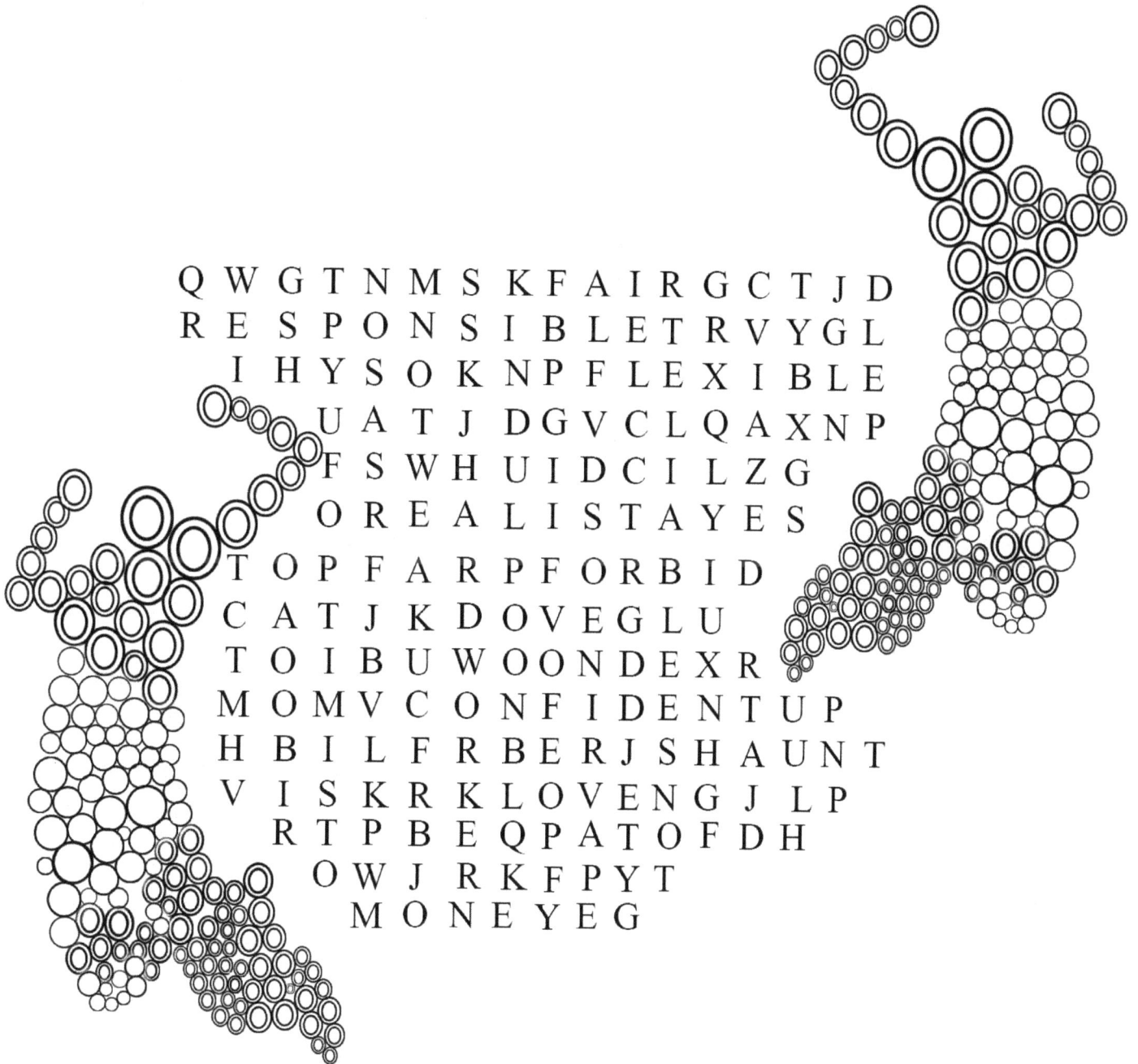

```
Q W G T N M S K F A I R G C T J D
R E S P O N S I B L E T R V Y G L
  I H Y S O K N P F L E X I B L E
    U A T J D G V C L Q A X N P
    F S W H U I D C I L Z G
    O R E A L I S T A Y E S
  T O P F A R P F O R B I D
  C A T J K D O V E G L U
  T O I B U W O O N D E X R
  M O M V C O N F I D E N T U P
  H B I L F R B E R J S H A U N T
  V I S K R K L O V E N G J L P
  R T P B E Q P A T O F D H
    O W J R K F P Y T
      M O N E Y E G
```

1. Confident	4. Hard worker	7. Kind
2. Optimist	5. Fair	8. Not weak
3. Flexible	6. Responsible	9. Realist

Connet--The--Dot

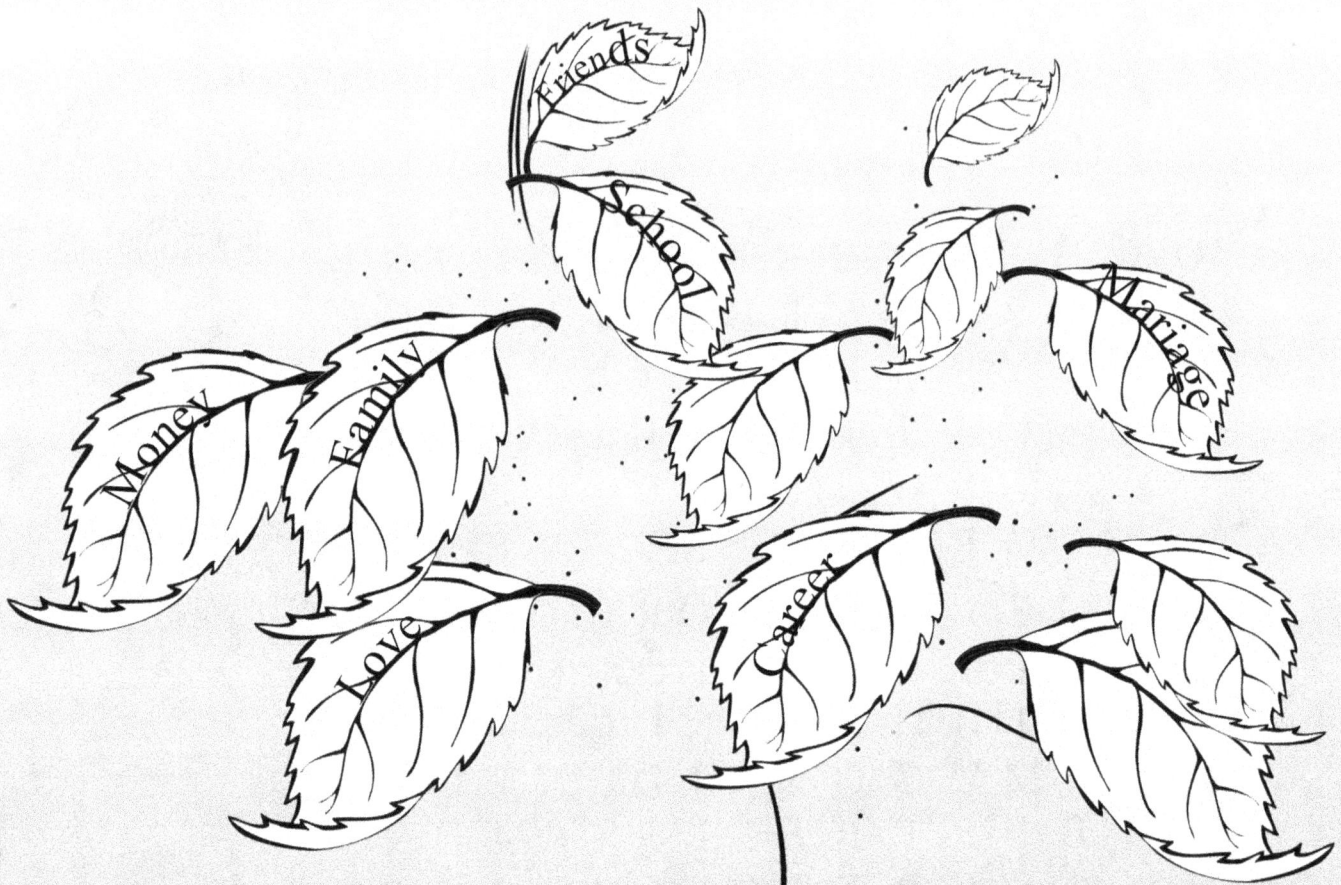

Friends

School

Money

Family

Love

Mariage

Career

1- Connect the dots
2- Color the leaf that has your goal
3- Add your own goal on the blank leaves
4- Make sure to achieve your goal IN YOUR LIFE.
   BECASUE YOU CAN!

IF YOU WANT SOMETHING YOU'VE NEVER HAD- YOU HAVE TO DO SOMETHING YOU'VE NEVER DONE...

Thomas Jefferson

What's the

Can you find and list the characteristics of a successful person VS unsuccessful?

List the characteristics that you think
goes under Group A-Winner or B-non achiever

Disciplined,
Take responsibility,
not ambitious,
Positive thinkers,

Strong will power,
Quit before sweat,
Closed minded,
Eager to learn,

Work hard,
Not confident,
Take action,
Do not set goals.

A

1- _____

2- _____

3- _____

4- _____

5- _____

6- _____

7- _____

difference?

Stop Saying I Wish
Start Saying I WILL
BE A WINNER
NOT A LOSER !

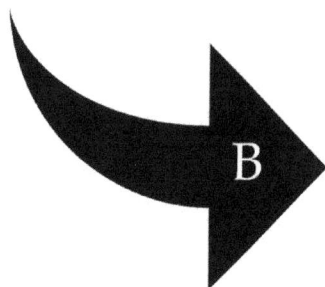

1- _____

2- _____

3- _____

4- _____

5- _____

Can you unscramble the words?

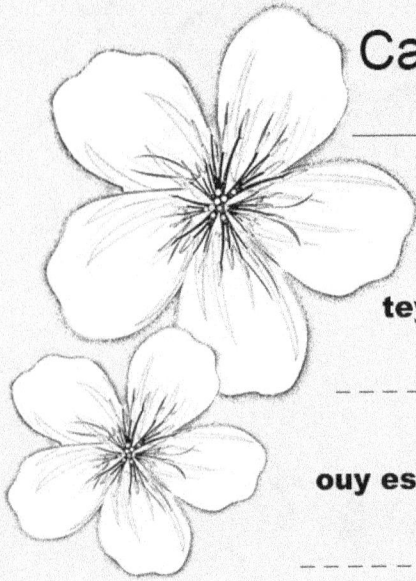

teyh genior oyu adn nhikt ouy an'tc ahievec ti

‑ ‑

ouy esqtioun eouryslf nda edep odnw oyu onkw ouy acn

‑ ‑

oyu akte het lcalenhge nad geibn rkiwngo ahdr no ouyr loag

‑ ‑

oyu on'dt vieg pu nvee fi ouy afil ta irfst

‑ ‑

keep going and be persistent

tnhiong acn sopt uyo eabusce oyu onwk ehetr's ontingh etbter athn esegin oueyrslf ucscede

‑ ‑

ist' otn asey utb ist' hortw it

‑ ‑

oyu rae het eky to ouyr ucssces!

‑ ‑

NOW LET'S DO THIS !!!

NEVER STOP
DOING YOUR BEST
JUST BECAUSE
SOMEONE DOESN'T
GIVE YOU CREDIT

Draw
connecting each quote
Movie or

1. It ain't about how hard you hit, it's about how hard you can get hit and keep moving

2. For what it's worth, it's never too late to be whoever you want to be

3. Don't tell me I can't do it, don't tell me it can't be done

4. Don't let anyone ever make you feel like you don't deserve what you want

What is your all time

_____

_____

_____

a line
to its corresponding
Actor

- **Howard Hughes**   - Aviator

- **Patrick Verona**   - 10 things I hate about you

- **Benjamin Button**   - The Curious Case

- **Rocky Balboa**   - Rocky

favorite movie quote?

_____

_____

_____

COLOR the LYRICS
SONG iS it? FILL iN the

Do you like coming up with the continuation of the

What __ _____

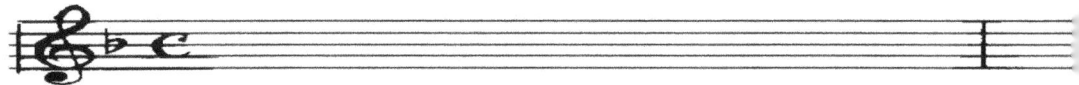

1

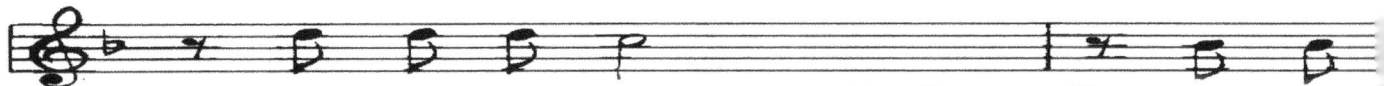

2 RED ROS- ES TOO, I SEE

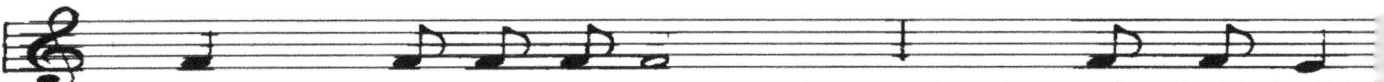

3 THINK to My- SeLF WHAT A WON

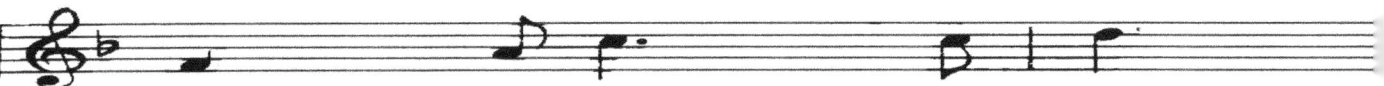

4 SKIES OF BL.UE and CLOUdS OF WHite

5 DARK Sacred NiGHt AND I ___

_____

_____

_____

aNd gueSS WHat

LaNK iN tHe titLe & iN LiNe 5

your own lyrics? write down
song in your own words!

_____ **World**

I SEE TREES OF GREEN

EM BLOOM For Me and you, AND I

RFUL WORLD I See

IE BRIGHT BLESSED DAY tHe

_ _ _ _ _ _ _ _ _ _ _ _ _ _ _

_ _ _ _ _

_____

_____

Let's match the ... in column A ... name of the person

1- "I have not failed. I've just found 10,000 ways that won't work."

2- "The difference between a successful person and others is not a lack of strength, not a lack of knowledge, but rather a lack of will."

3- "It is never too late to be what you might have been."

4- "An obstacle is often a stepping stone."

5- "All our dreams can come true, if we have the courage to pursue them."

6- "Success is the ability to go from one failure to another with no loss of enthusiasm."

Do you have ... why don't you add it to the

7- _____

famous sayings
with the
that belongs to

A- GEORGE ELIOT

B- WALT DISNEY

C- VINCE LOMBARDI

D- THOMAS A. EDISON

E- WILLIAM PRESCOTT

F- WINSTON CHURCHILL

Pessimism will take you nowhere. Hard work, Love, Hope, Passion, and Focus will help you succeed. However, Persistence is the ultimate route for your long term success.

your own quote?
famous people's quote list?

G- _____

Can you find the ultimate route to Long Term Success?

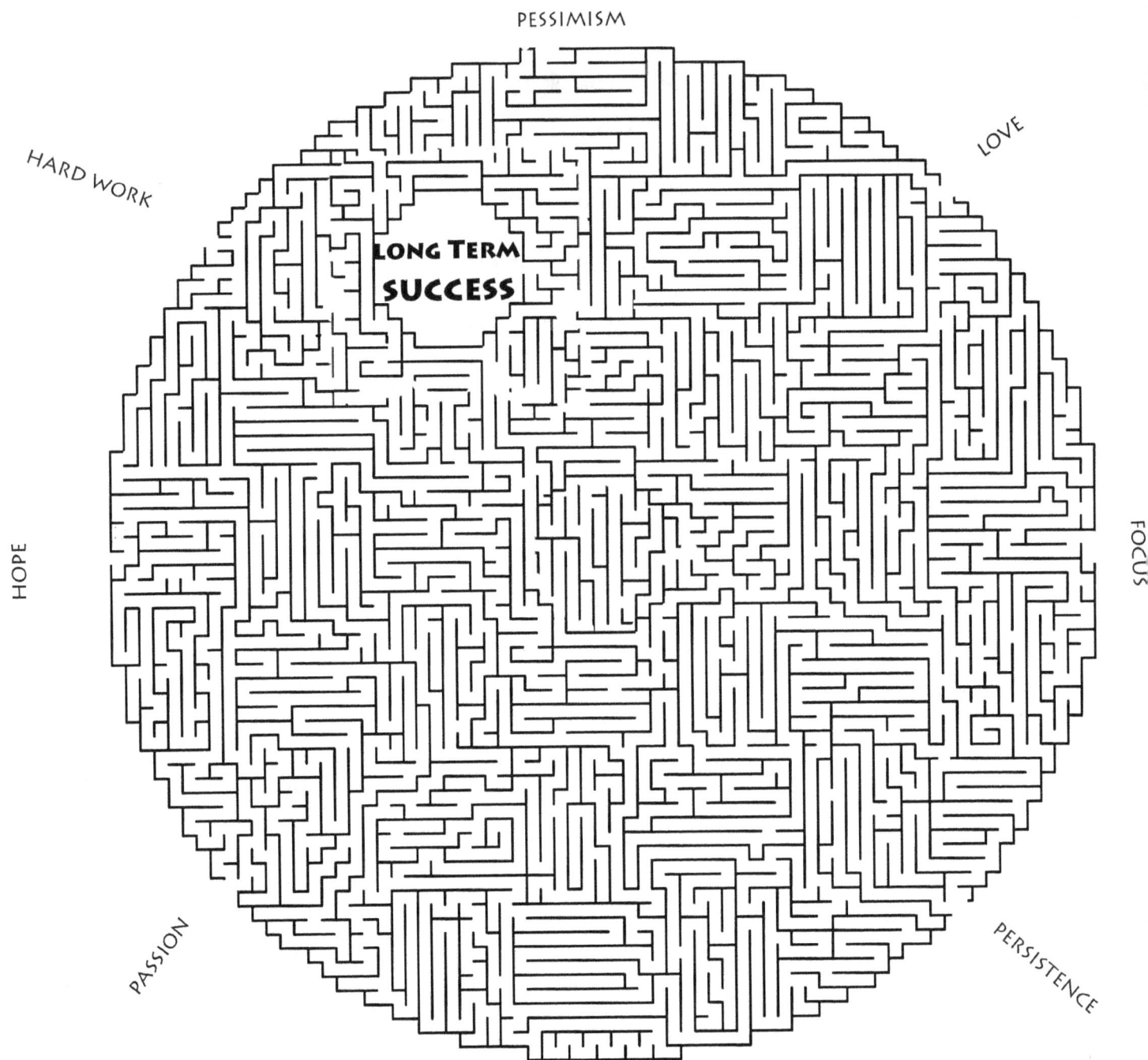

PESSIMISM

LOVE

HARD WORK

LONG TERM SUCCESS

HOPE

FOCUS

PASSION

PERSISTENCE

DO YOU THINK HE GAVE UP?

Abraham Lincoln ...

1832: Lost Job
1833: Failed in Business
1835: His sweetheart died
1836: Had nervous breakdown
1838: Defeated for speaker

1849: Rejected for land officer
1854: Defeated for U.S. Senate
1856: Defeated for nomination for Vice President
1858: Again defeated for U.S. Senate

1860: ELECTED PRESIDENT!

Abraham Lincoln changed the world by ending the slavery. What if he gave up in 1859?? Great people never give up! Will you?

Always remember this saying " if you are going through hell, Keep Going"!

By Winston Churchill

Failing is not shameful, giving up is. List your failures like above. Write your success only after you earn it!

1- _____

2- _____

3- _____

4- _____

5- _____

6- _____

7- _____

8- _____

9- _____

My Success: DATE: _____   DESCRIBE: _____

SUCCEED

ICAN

IWILLSUCCE

IWATCH

IWILLSUCCE

ICANSUCCE

Hint: Find out each word and color each in differ-
ent color. Once you're done think about a specific
goal that you want to achieve, close your eyes and
say the words that you just colored slowly and with
confidence.
Because YOU can! Because YOU will!!!

ICANSUCCEED
DIWILLSUCCEED
HESUCCEED
HESUCCEED
DIWILLSUCCEED
DICANSU

Use Your

You decided to step out and achieve your goals!
What are

Imagination

What's the crowd saying about you?
your thoughts?

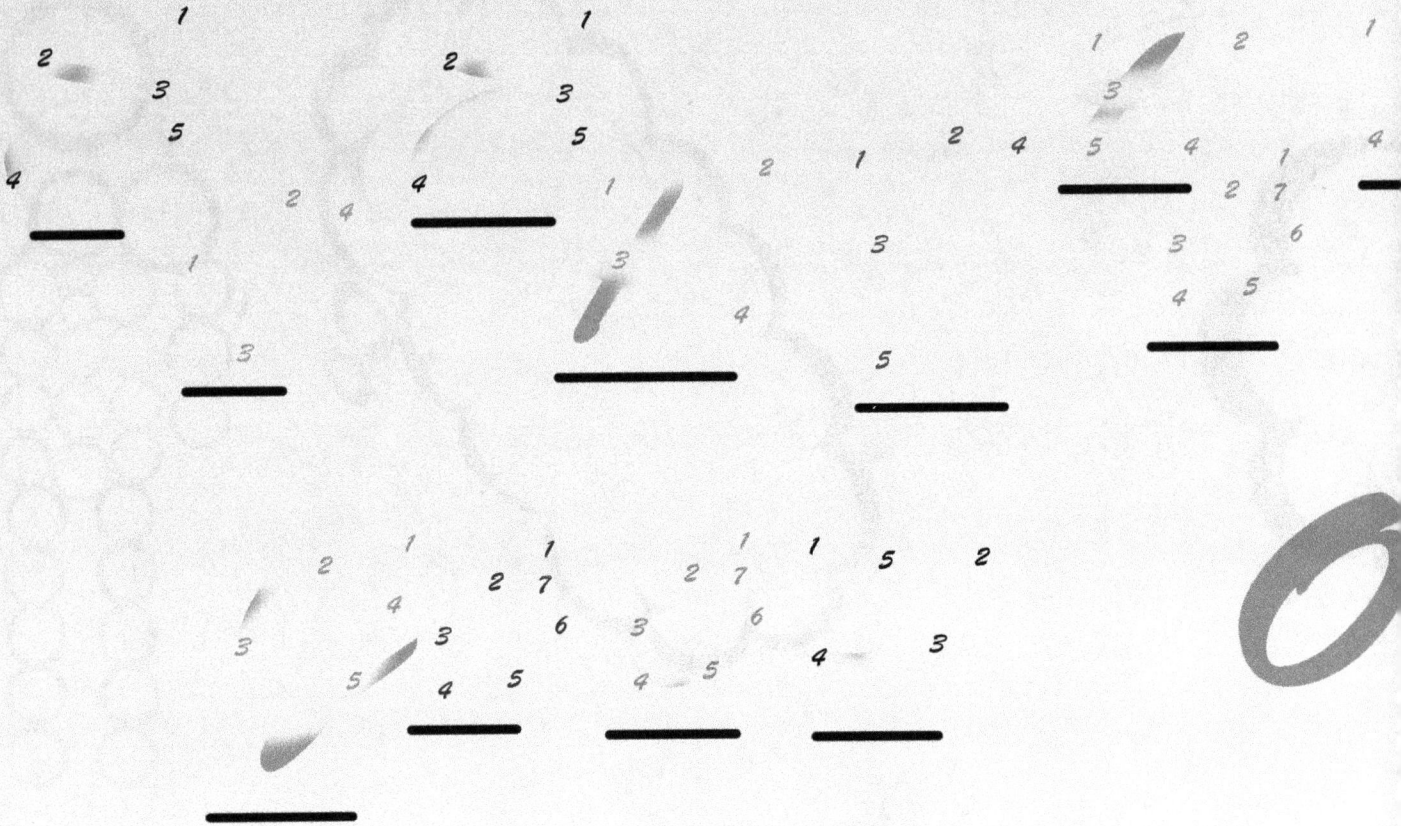

the numbers
numbers in each letter
the hidden quote!!

Can Be

NLY

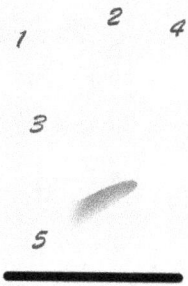

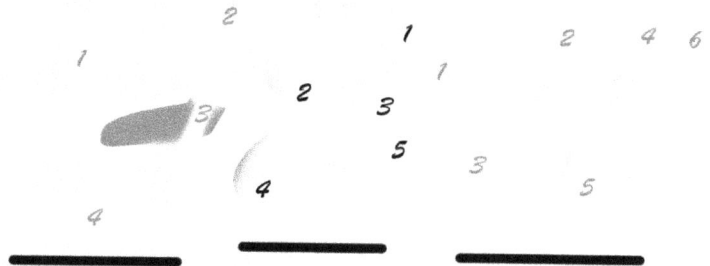

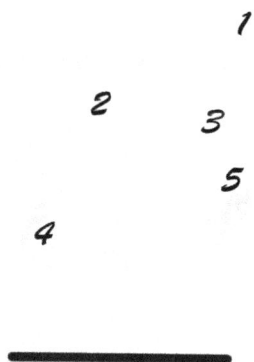

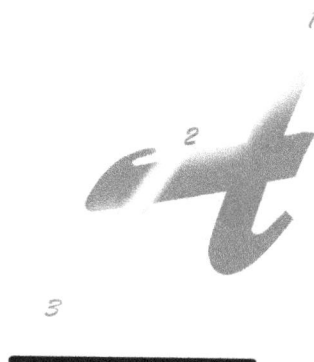

Are you one of the few??

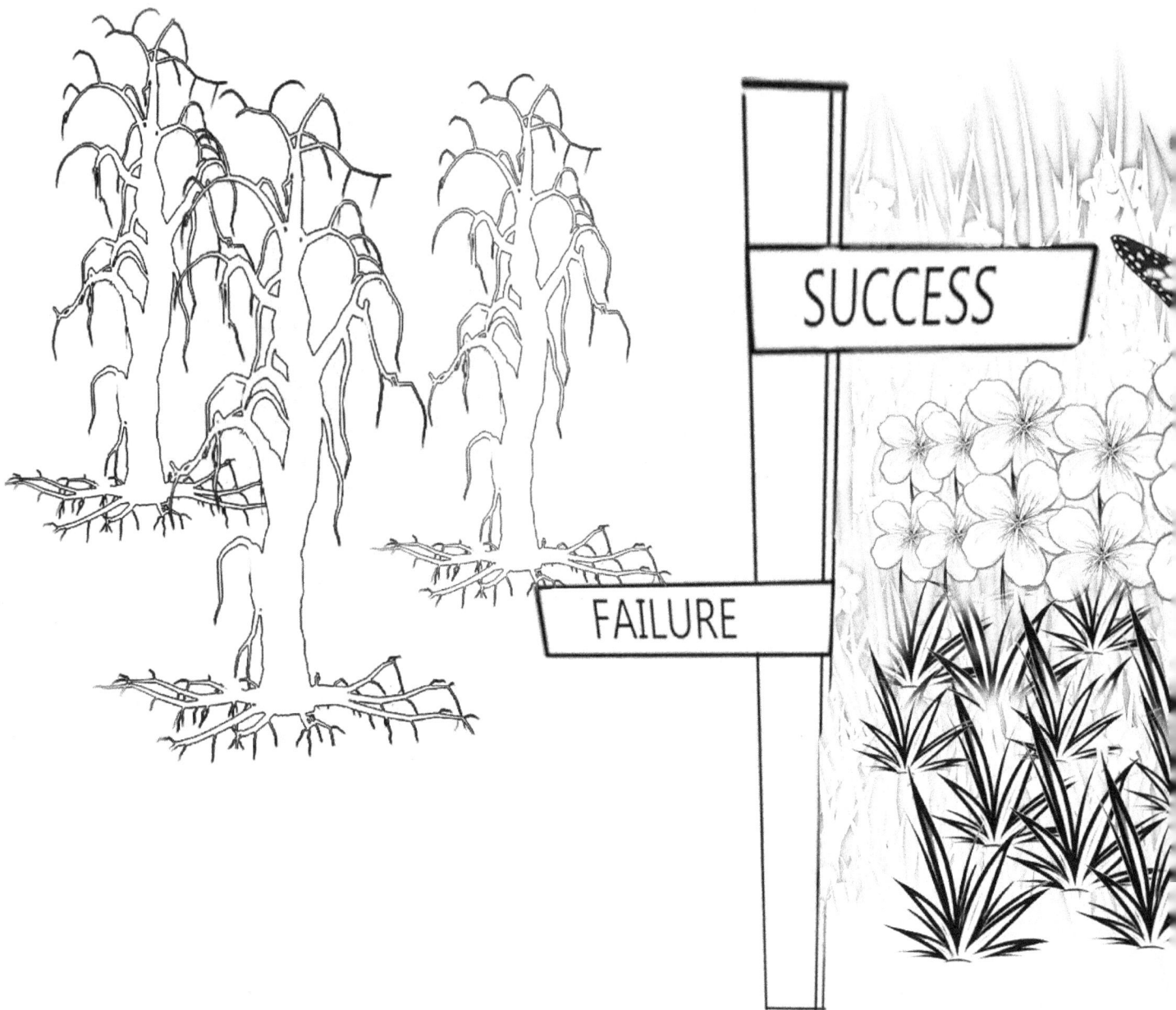

Close your eyes and pretend that you have already achieved th
there! You have succeeded and you know you did it! Describe
How do you feel about yourself? What does your family and

goal that you have always dreamed about. You're finally
the feeling, how does it feel like living your dream?
friends think about you?

Awaken Your inner Tsunami

How did you achieve your goal?
Write down the plan that you followed and succeeded.
Are you ready to follow the plan?

Answers

Page 8:

Successful Person	Unsuccessful person
• Disciplined	• Not Ambitious
• Take Responsibility	• Quit Before Sweat
• Positive Thinkers	• Closed Minded
• Work Hard	• Not Confident
• Take Action	• Do Not Set Goals
• Strong Will Power	
• Eager to Learn	

Page 10:

- They ignore you and think you can't achieve it
- You question yourself and deep down you know can
- You take the challenge and begin working on your goal
- You don't give up even if you fail at first
- Nothing can stop you because you know there's nothing better than seeing yourself succeed
- It's not easy but it's worth it
- You are the key to your success

Page 14:

1-   Rocky Balboa
2-   Benjamin Button
3-   Howard Hughes
4-   Patrick Verona

Page 18:

1-D
2-C
3-A
4-E
5-B
6-F

Page 22:

Pessimism will take you nowhere. Hard work, Love, Hope, Passion, and Focus will help you succeed. However, Persistence is the ultimate route for your long term success.

Page 26:

Everybody can be good only few can be great.